W9-BAT-014

LANGUAGE ARTS

EXPLORER JUNIOR

How to Write a Fairy Tale

by Cecilia Minden
and Kate Roth

Published in the United States of America by Cherry Lake Publishing
Ann Arbor, Michigan
www.cherrylakepublishing.com

Content Adviser: Jeannette Mancilla-Martinez, EdD, Assistant Professor of
Literacy, Language, and Culture, University of Illinois at Chicago

Design and Illustration: The Design Lab

Photo Credit: Page 8, ©iStockphot.com/wibs24.

Library of Congress Cataloging-in-Publication Data
Minden, Cecilia.
 How to write a fairy tale/by Cecilia Minden and Kate Roth.
 p. cm. — (Language Arts Explorer Junior)
 Includes bibliographical references and index.
 ISBN 978-1-61080-309-0 (lib. bdg.)—ISBN 978-1-61080-314-4
(e-book)—ISBN 978-1-61080-319-9 (pbk.)
 1. Fairy tales—Authorship—Juvenile literature. I. Roth, Kate. II. Title.
III. Series.
 PN3377.5.F32M56 2012
 808.06'6398—dc23 2011031709

Cherry Lake Publishing would like to acknowledge the work
of The Partnership for 21st Century Skills. Please visit
www.21stcenturyskills.org for more information.

Printed in the United States of America
Corporate Graphics Inc.
January 2012
CLSP10

Table of Contents

CHAPTER ONE

Once upon a Time in a Faraway Village

Pigs don't really talk, but in a fairy tale they can.

Have you ever read *The Three Little Pigs*? It is a **fairy tale**. Fairy tales are fantasies. They take place in a make-believe time and place. They usually begin with the words "Once upon a time."

In every fairy tale **characters** have magical powers. For example, animals can talk or people can make things change shape. Fairy tales tell stories of good against **evil**. Good always wins.

Fairy tales are fun to write because you can use your **imagination** to create a whole new world. Ready to give it a try?

One of the first things you must decide is the fairy tale's setting. Maybe you want your fairy tale to take place at an old bridge or a county fair. It might be in a castle or a cottage in the forest. Remember, it can't take place somewhere real like your city or school.

A long fairy tale can have more than one setting.

Choose Your Setting

HERE'S WHAT YOU'LL NEED:
- Pencil
- Paper

INSTRUCTIONS:
1. Write the title "Planning Sheet" on the top of your paper. You will be planning your story on this paper.
2. Make a list of places where your fairy tale can take place.
3. Be sure the places are not real places.
4. Choose one place from your list for the setting of your story.

To get a copy of this activity, visit www.cherrylakepublishing.com/activities.

PLANNING SHEET

Setting ideas:
- castle
- cottage in the woods
- wooden bridge
- county fair

CHAPTER TWO

There Were Three Pigs and a Wolf

Next you will add your characters. You must have both good and evil characters. You can use humans or animals. You could also use fantasy characters. Elves, fairies, and dragons often appear in fairy tales. You can combine two kinds of characters to make a new one. For example, you could write about a horse with wings.

A mermaid is a fantasy character because she is part girl and part fish.

Picture your characters in your mind. What do they look like? What are their names? Do they have magic powers? What do we know about them? In *The Three Little Pigs*, we know that each pig wants to build his own house. You will also include dialogue. Think about how your characters sound when they talk.

Good characters draw you into the story.

Choose Your Characters

HERE'S WHAT YOU'LL NEED:
- Pencil
- The Planning Sheet you started in the first activity
- A fresh sheet of paper

INSTRUCTIONS:

PART ONE—DESCRIBE YOUR CHARACTERS

1. Choose at least three characters for your fairy tale. Make one character evil. Make one good. Make one with magical powers.
2. Write a list of your characters on your Planning Sheet.
3. Describe each character. How do they look? How do they sound when they speak? Are they good or evil? Do they have magical powers?

CONTINUED

To get a copy of this activity, visit www.cherrylakepublishing.com/activities.

PLANNING SHEET

Setting ideas:
- castle
- cottage in the woods
- wooden bridge
- county fair

Character ideas:
- Tom, a brave young knight in search of the Terrible Dragon Gnik
- Zia, a pretty cat who can sing
- The Terrible Dragon Gnik who guards the gate to the castle

(CHOOSE YOUR CHARACTERS CONTINUED)

PART TWO—BEGIN YOUR STORY

1. Write a title for your fairy tale on your fresh sheet of paper. This is your Story Sheet.
2. Write the beginning of your story. Begin with the words "Once upon a time."
3. Write a few sentences that describe your setting and your characters.
4. Include some dialogue. This will help your readers imagine how your characters sound when they are talking.

The Terrible Dragon Gnik

Once upon a time, there lived a knight named Tom. He was riding to a castle to slay the Terrible Dragon Gnik when he saw a pretty cat in the middle of the road. The cat was purring, but it sounded more like singing.

"Please come with me, little singing cat," Tom said. "You will be good company." She jumped very high and landed on the back of Tom's horse. "You can jump very high," said Tom. "You are a cat who can do many things."

The knight, his horse, and the cat went galloping down the road.

CHAPTER THREE

The Wolf Wanted to Eat the Pigs

Now it is time to put the characters in **conflict** with each other. The evil character wants the good character to do something that causes harm. For example, the wolf wants the little pig to let him in the house. If the pig lets him in, the wolf will eat him. The pig has to think of a way to **outsmart** the wolf.

Fairy tales often use the number three, as in three wishes or three tries to do something. The wolf tries to get to the pigs three times.

Think of different ways your characters will be in conflict. What does the evil one want the good one to do? How can the good one stop the evil one?

Choose Your Conflict

HERE'S WHAT YOU'LL NEED:
- A pencil
- Your Planning Sheet
- Your Story Sheet

To get a copy of this activity, visit www.cherrylakepublishing.com/activities.

INSTRUCTIONS:
1. Write the word "Conflict" on your Planning Sheet.
2. Write a sentence or two about what the conflict will be. Think about how the evil character wants to harm the good character.
3. Continue adding to your story on your Story Sheet.
4. Write about the conflict.
5. Include dialogue so your readers can see how your characters talk to each other.

PLANNING SHEET

Setting ideas:
- castle
- cottage in the woods
- wooden bridge
- county fair

Character ideas:
- Tom, a brave young knight in search of the Terrible Dragon Gnik
- Zia, a pretty cat who can sing
- The Terrible Dragon Gnik who guards the gate to the castle

Conflict:
- The dragon is blocking the castle door. He won't let anyone in or out. The people in the castle are starving. It is up to Tom the Knight to save them.

The Terrible Dragon Gnik

Once upon a time, there lived a knight named Tom. He was riding to a castle to slay the Terrible Dragon Gnik when he saw a pretty cat in the middle of the road. The cat was purring, but it sounded more like singing.

"Please come with me, little singing cat," Tom said. "You will be good company." She jumped very high and landed on the back of Tom's horse. "You can jump very high," said Tom. "You are a cat who can do many things."

The knight, his horse, and the cat went galloping down the road.

The Terrible Dragon Gnik stood at the gate of the castle. He wouldn't let anyone in, and he wouldn't let anyone out. People in the castle would soon starve to death. Other knights had tried to slay the dragon, but Gnik always won the battle. Tom rode up to the castle door.

"What must I do to get into the castle?" asked Tom.

The Terrible Dragon Gnik smiled an evil smile.

"Sing my favorite song," said Gnik. "You get three tries to get it right."

Tom thought and thought. There were so many songs. Which one could it be? First, he tried a simple tune he'd learned as a child. "WRONG!" roared the dragon. The cat began purring. "Be quiet, little cat," said Tom. "I'm trying to think."

Second, he tried a song he learned in school. It was a happy tune that he'd always liked. "WRONG, again!" roared the dragon. Now the cat was purring louder. "Quiet!" said Tom.

Tom had only one chance left. What could he do?

CHAPTER FOUR

The Pigs Tricked the Wolf

Finally, you write your solution.
You solve the conflict between good and bad.
Perhaps a fairy godmother suddenly appears.
Maybe a flying horse comes in the window.
Some fairy tales use tricks. For example, the
pigs trick the wolf into falling into a pot of
boiling water. Use your imagination!

ACTIVITY

Choose the Solution

HERE'S WHAT YOU'LL NEED:
- A pencil
- Your Planning Sheet
- Your Story Sheet

CONTINUED

To get a copy of this activity, visit
www.cherrylakepublishing.com/activities.

ACTIVITY

(CHOOSE THE SOLUTION CONTINUED)

INSTRUCTIONS:

1. Write the word "Solution" on your Planning Sheet.
2. Plan the solution to the conflict. How will the good character win out over the evil character?
3. Continue adding to your story on your Story Sheet.
4. Write about how the characters solve their problem.
5. Use dialogue.

PLANNING SHEET

Setting ideas:

- castle
- cottage in the woods
- wooden bridge
- county fair

Character ideas:

- Tom, a brave young knight in search of the Terrible Dragon Gnik
- Zia, a pretty cat who can sing
- The Terrible Dragon Gnik who guards the gate to the castle

Conflict:

- The dragon is blocking the castle door. He won't let anyone in or out. The people in the castle are starving. It is up to Tom the Knight to save them.

Solution:

- The cat purrs "Happy Birthday." The dragon becomes a king, and the cat becomes a princess.

The Terrible Dragon Gnik

Once upon a time, there lived a knight named Tom. He was riding to a
... Dragon Gnik when he saw a pretty cat in the

Tom noticed that the cat's purring sounded like "Happy Birthday."
Could that be it? Tom took a deep breath. This was his last chance.
What if he got it wrong?

"Happy birthday to you," sang Tom. The Terrible Dragon Gnik stood
very still. He started growing smaller and smaller. Soon the dragon was
gone. In his place stood the King.

"Thank you, thank you, good knight," said the King. "An evil wizard
cast a spell on me and my castle. I was to remain a dragon until
someone sang my favorite song. How did you know what it was?"

"My cat," said Tom. But the cat had turned into a beautiful princess.
"I am Princess Zia," she said. "I was also under the wizard's spell, but I
jumped over the fence and went for help."

CHAPTER FIVE

The Wolf Ran Away

The ending to your fairy tale can be short. You want the readers to know what happened. For example, what happens after the wolf falls in the pot of boiling water? If you read the story, you know. He jumps out and runs away. This shows how the good pigs get rid of the evil wolf.

Fairy tales often have a **moral** to the story. This means that a lesson is learned. The pigs learned not to build houses out of sticks or straw. What can we learn from your fairy tale?

ACTIVITY

Choose the Ending

HERE'S WHAT YOU'LL NEED:
- A pencil
- Your Planning Sheet
- Your Story Sheet

To get a copy of this activity, visit www.cherrylakepublishing.com/activities.

CONTINUED

(CHOOSE THE ENDING CONTINUED)

INSTRUCTIONS:

1. Write the word "Ending" on your Planning Sheet.
2. Write a sentence or two about the ending of your story.
3. Continue adding to your story on your Story Sheet.
4. Write an ending that tells your readers what happened after the conflict was solved.

PLANNING SHEET

Setting ideas:
- castle
- cottage in the woods
- wooden bridge
- county fair

Character ideas:
- Tom, a brave young knight in search of the Terrible Dragon Gnik
- Zia, a pretty cat who can sing
- The Terrible Dragon Gnik who guards the gate to the castle

Conflict:
- The dragon is blocking the castle door. He won't let anyone in or out. The people in the castle are starving. It is up to Tom the knight to save them.

Solution:
- The cat purrs "Happy Birthday." The dragon becomes a king, and the cat becomes a princess.

Ending:
- The characters have a party and sing "Happy Birthday" to everybody.

The Terrible Dragon Gnik

Once upon a time, there lived a knight named Tom. He was riding to a
... Dragon Gnik when he saw a pretty cat in the

Tom noticed that the cat's purring sounded like "Happy Birthday."
Could that be it? Tom took a deep breath. This was his last chance.
What if he got it wrong?

"Happy birthday to you," sang Tom. The Terrible Dragon Gnik stood
very still. He started growing smaller and smaller. Soon the dragon was
gone. In his place stood the King.

"Thank you, thank you, good knight," said the King. "An evil wizard
cast a spell on me and my castle. I was to remain a dragon until
someone sang my favorite song. How did you know what it was?"

"My cat," said Tom. But the cat had turned into a
beautiful princess. "I am Princess Zia," she said.
"I was also under the wizard's spell, but I jumped
over the fence and went for help."

"Open the doors," said the King. "Let us give
thanks to this brave knight and clever
Princess Zia. Together they saved our
castle. Let us bring in food for a great party.
We will all dance and sing. We will sing
'Happy Birthday' to everybody!"

CHAPTER SIX

The Pigs Lived Happily Ever After

The last lines in your fairy tale are important.
Most fairy tales end with the same two lines.
  "And they lived happily ever after.
  The End."

A Final Look at Your Fairy Tale

Read your story aloud to hear how it sounds.
Then ask yourself these questions:

☐ YES ☐ NO Did I begin with "Once upon a time"?

☐ YES ☐ NO Did I use a fairy tale setting?

☐ YES ☐ NO Did I include a title?

☐ YES ☐ NO Did I include a conflict between good and evil?

☐ YES ☐ NO Did I include a solution?

☐ YES ☐ NO Did I close with "And they lived happily ever after. The End."?

☐ YES ☐ NO Did I use correct grammar and spelling?

The Terrible Dragon Gnik

Once upon a time, there lived a knight named Tom. He was riding to a ...Dragon Gnik when he saw a pretty cat in the...

Tom noticed that the cat's purring sounded like "Happy Birthday." Could that be it? Tom took a deep breath. This was his last chance. What if he got it wrong?

"Happy birthday to you," sang Tom. The Terrible Dragon Gnik stood very still. He started growing smaller and smaller. Soon the dragon was gone. In his place stood the King.

"Thank you, thank you, good knight," said the King. "An evil wizard cast a spell on me and my castle. I was to remain a dragon until someone sang my favorite song. How did you know what it was?"

"My cat," said Tom. But the cat had turned into a beautiful princess. "I am Princess Zia," she said. "I was also under the wizard's spell, but I jumped over the fence and went for help."

"Open the doors," said the King. "Let us give thanks to this brave knight and clever Princess Zia. Together they saved our castle. Let us bring in food for a great party. We will all dance and sing. We will sing 'Happy Birthday' to everybody!"

And they lived happily ever after.

The End.

Glossary

characters (KAR-ik-turz) people in a story, book, play, movie, or television show

conflict (KAHN-flikt) a clash or disagreement between people

dialogue (DYE-uh-log) conversation in a story, play, or movie

evil (EE-vuhl) very bad and mean

fairy tale (FAIR-ee TAYL) a fantasy story set in a make-believe time and place

fantasies (FAN-tuh-seez) stories with magical characters or strange places or events

imagination (i-maj-uh-NAY-shuhn) the ability to form pictures in your mind of things that are not real

moral (MOR-uhl) a lesson taught by a story

outsmart (out-SMART) to win out over someone else by being very clever

setting (SET-ing) the place where the events of a story happen

solution (suh-LOO-shuhn) the answer to a problem

For More Information

BOOKS

Andersen, Hans Christian. *The Fairy Tales of Hans Christian Andersen.* New York: Simon & Brown, 2011.

Warren, Celia. *How to Write Stories.* Laguna Hills, CA: QEB Publishers, 2007.

WEB SITES

Fun English Games—Story Writing Game for Kids
www.funenglishgames.com/writinggames/story.html
Explore this site that will help you write better stories.

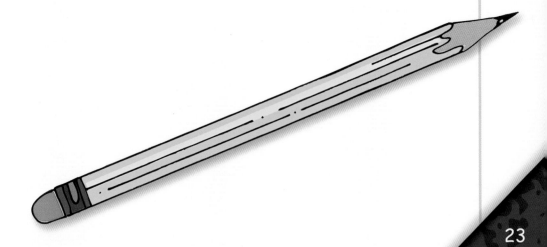

Index

About the Authors

Cecilia Minden, PhD, is the former director of the Language and Literacy Program at Harvard Graduate School of Education. She earned her doctorate from the University of Virginia. While at Harvard, Dr. Minden also taught several writing courses. Her research focuses on early literacy skills and developing phonics curriculums. She is now a full-time literacy consultant and the author of more than 100 books for children. Dr. Minden lives with her family in Chapel Hill, North Carolina. She likes to write early in the morning while the house is still quiet.

Kate Roth has a doctorate from Harvard University in language and literacy and a master's degree from Columbia University Teachers College in curriculum and teaching. Her work focuses on writing instruction in the primary grades. She has taught kindergarten, first grade, and Reading Recovery. She has also instructed hundreds of teachers from around the world in early literacy practices. She lives in Shanghai, China, with her husband and three children, ages 3, 7, and 10. Together they do a lot of writing to stay in touch with friends and family and to record their experiences.